DRIFTING FLOWERS

By
SADAKICHI HARTMANN

Illustrated

PUBLIC DOMAIN POETS

Editor: Dick Whyte —: No. X :— October 2022

SADAKICHI HARTMANN (1867-1944) was born to a Japanese mother and German father on the island of Dejima, off the coast of Nagasaki. His mother died giving birth to his brother, and they were sent to Germany soon after to live with relatives. Hartmann's father enrolled him in the navy as a teenager, so he ran away to Paris, which prompted his father to disown him. Hartmann was then sent to Philadelphia to live with an uncle, and it was there he became interested in the arts. In the mid-1890s he self-published his first dramatic works, and a book of conversations with Walt Whitman – one of the earliest English-language 'free verse' poets – whom he had recently befriended. In the 1900s Hartmann began writing poetry, drawing influence from Whitman and French symbolism, alongside Japanese poetics, and in 1904 he self-published the earliest known set of English-language tanka, alongside a short essay on tanka and haikai. In the 1910s he followed this up with *My Rubaiyat*, a sequence of linked tanka-esque blank-verse, inspired by the *Rubaiyat of Omar Khayyam*, and became friends with experimental writers like Gertrude Stein and Ezra Pound. Hartmann's final book of poetry, *Tanka & Haikai: Japanese Rhythms* (1916), remains one of the earliest published standalone collections of English-language tanka and haikai, followed by Noguchi's *Japanese Hokkus* (1920), and Jun Fujita's *Tanka: Poems in Exile* (1923).

Tanka & Haikai: Japanese Rhythms (self-published, 1916); 'Some New Haikai' (*Greenwich Village*, July 1915); with selections from *My Rubaiyat* (Mangan Printing Company, 1913); *Drifting Flowers of the Sea & Other Verses* (self-published, 1904); 'Why I Publish My Own Books' (*Greenwich Village*, Nov. 1915); & 'The Japanese Conception of Poetry' [edited] (*The Reader*, Jan. 1904).

Cover: Tosa School – 'Spring Orchid', & Hokusai – 'Mt. Fushiyama'; also Motonobu – 'Mountain Stream', Yamoto-Tosa School – 'Autumn Flowers', & 'Cranes' (interior), from Hartmann's *Japanese Art* (L.C. Page & Co., 1904). Inside: Hartmann – 'Self Portrait' (from *Japanese Rhythms*), 'Photo' (from *My Rubaiyat*); LB – 'Drawings of Hartmann' (*Greenwich Village*, Nov. 1915); & various ornaments from Hartmann's *Conversations with Walt Whitman* (self-published, 1895), etc.

This collection ©2022. All individual poems, illustrations, and ornaments belong to the 'public domain', unless otherwise noted, and may be freely copied and/or distributed. Some elements of the originals may have been marginally edited, for clarity and consistency.

PUBLIC DOMAIN PRESS
Aotearoa / New Zealand
ISBN: 978-1-99-117769-8 (print) • 978-1-99-117764-3 (pdf)
978-1-99-117767-4 (kindle)

SADAKICHI HARTMANN
DRIFTING FLOWERS & OTHER VERSES

JAPANESE RHYTHMS

The entirety of Hartmann's final book of poetry,
Tanka & Haikai: Japanese Rhythms (1916).

MY RUBAIYAT

Selections from Hartmann's blank-verse sequence,
inspired by the *Rubaiyat of Omar Khayyam* (1913).

DRIFTING FLOWERS

Selections from Hartmann's first book of poetry,
Drifting Flowers of the Sea (1904).

CONCEPTIONS OF POETRY

Selections from 'Why I Publish My Own Books' (1915)
& 'The Japanese Conception of Poetry' (1904).

SADAKICHI HARTMANN
TANKA AND HAIKAI

Japanese Rhythms

AUTHOR'S EDITION

SAN FRANCISCO, 1916

Published previously in
The Reader, The Stylus,
and Bruno's Chap Books.

Edition limited to 200
copies.

Copyrighted, 1916,
By Sadakichi Hartmann

TANKA I.

WINTER? Spring? Who knows?
   White buds from the plumtrees wing
And mingle with the snows.
No blue skies these flowers bring,
Yet their fragrance augurs Spring.

The Tanka (short poem) is the most popular and characteristic of the various forms of Japanese poetry. It consists of five lines of 5, 7, 5, 7, and 7 syllables—31 syllables in all. The addition of the rhyme is original with the author.

TANKA II.

OH, were the white waves,
    Far on the glimmering sea
That the moonshine laves,
Dream flowers drifting to me,—
I would cull them, love, for thee.

TANKA III.

Moon, somnolent, white,
  Mirrored in a waveless sea,
What fickle mood of night
Urged thee from heaven to flee
And live in the dawnlit sea?

TANKA IV.

Like mist on the lees,
 Fall gently, oh rain of Spring
On the orange trees
That to Ume's casement cling—
Perchance, she'll hear the love-bird sing.

TANKA V.

THOUGH love has grown cold
   The woods are bright with flowers,
Why not as of old
Go to the wildwood bowers
And dream of—bygone hours!

TANKA VI.

TELL, what name beseems
   These vain and wandering days!
Like the bark of dreams
That from souls at daybreak strays
They are lost on trackless ways.

TANKA VII.

OH, climb to my lips,
    Frail muse of the amber wine!
Joy to him who sips
Cups of fragrant sake wine
Flowing from some fount divine.

TANKA VIII.

IF pleasures be mine
  As aeons and aeons roll by,
Why should I repine
That under some future sky
I may live as butterfly?

TANKA IX.

WERE we able to tell
    When old age would come our way,
We would muffle the bell,
Lock the door and go away—
Let him call some other day.

HAIKAI I.

WHITE petals afloat
 On a winding woodland stream—
What else is life's dream!

The Haikai is a Tanka minus the concluding fourteen syllables. It was favored in the sixteenth century. Frequently it is purely poetical and the association of thought produced too vague to be conveyed in English with such exaggerated brevity.

HAIKAI II.

Butterflies a—wing—
 Are your flowers returning
To your branch in Spring.

HAIKAI III.

At new moon we met!
  Two weeks I've waited in vain.
To-night!—Don't forget.

HAIKAI IV.

OH, red maple leaves,
  There seem more of you these eves
Than ever grew on trees.

Some New Haikai
By Sadakichi Hartmann.

IF all the year round
    With blossoms the hills were white—
Would they seem less bright!

ON the barren cliff
    The fir for her roots finds room—
Love on naught may bloom.

HAVE all leaves turned red,
    Has summer past to tell me
That my youth has fled!

excerpts from My Rubaiyat by Sadakichi Hartmann

Of a poem of this scope and character, it can never be said that it is complete and finished. No doubt, it will be revised many times, but the poem has crystallized sufficiently in thought and versification to be offered to the public.

The rhythm may appear strange at times. To fully appreciate it, it would be necessary to hear the author read the poem. The metre is a combination of Whitman's free rhymeless rhythm, the *vers libre* which changes with every subject and mood, and the vague alliteration of sound in quarter tones, characteristic of Japanese poetry.

Was life once happier than
　　　　now?
Who is there to tell the story
Of the bliss of dim dead ages.
We know that roses still bloom,
Books and music still make
　　　us dream,
Why mourn o'er "snows of
　　　yesterdays"

Sex is a power all cherish,
We worship it on bended knees,
Like old wine it yields the
      magic
Of oblivion and ecstasies,
The moments drift on golden
      clouds
To regions of the white beyond.

The more we give the less we
                  gain—
This is a bitter truth to tell.
Yet passion is a fleeting thing
As flowers wane in summer's
                  heat,
Thus eager kisses, thigh to thigh
Turn phantoms with the colder
                  morn,

Love is a growth, a wondrous plant
That scatters its seed plots unseen,
That sheds rarest unknown
                  delights
To those few that worship the dream.
For love squanders all its treasures,
Why should it ask for a return.

Let me escape from the city
Into the blue shimmering night,
It speaks of all I could have
          loved,
It speaks of all I longed to see,
To understand, to own, and feel—
Why did so little come to me!

Ah, my fate is not different.
It is like that of all the rest.
There grew flowers at the wayside—
They were mine. I did not cull
          them.
There were chances made for
          blessing
When both of us remain'd unblessed

They skip o'er the gleaming
                surface,
They sink and vanish from sight
As all that abides on this earth.
Yet on the surface like stray
                thoughts
Each ripple owns an inner life
And wavelike stirs the azure
                brine.

One holy war has to be fought ~
To make both man and woman free:
The world will flash with signal
                lights,
Each land ring with its people's
           voice ~
For from those crimson rivulets
Will flow a saner better life.

What can we do, how can we help!
The poor can never help the poor,
The rich but scatter alms derived
From what is due the common herd.
The weed plots are crowded thick,
Who cuts a path for weary feet!

Oh, the helplessness of the aged,
Of the poor the sick, the lonely.
Can you explain why they suffer,
Must some perish while others
              thrive?
Is survival of the fittest
Due to the harshness of mankind?

How can I give right directions
When I am a wanderer myself?
Onward I stroll and ever on
In my own way courting the sun
And fashioning some paradise
Of passing winds and flying
        clouds.

You might not like such simple
        fare,
For you the winds may blow too
        mild~
I cannot tread your well-paved roads
Though verdant they may seem to you.
Each path leads to some point of
        view,
What you like best, is best for you.

To meet the hours as they come,
Salute the days as they pass by,
To bend your neck to no one's yoke,
To be full master of yourself,
To do a kindness when you can—
That is the happiness of life.

To help a friend in dire needs,
To speak a word to the oppressed,
To think of things that help
                  mankind,
To scatter joy, unasked, unblessed—
For knowing minds divine the rest—
That is the happiness of life.

There are roses and there is youth,
There are joys and sorrows and
	love,
Dawn and twilight, the noonday
	sun,
The rolling plains, the sky and
	the sea,
None have lost their old time
	mystery,
Events pass away, beauty
	survives.

DRIFTING FLOWERS OF THE SEA

AND OTHER POEMS

-by-

Sadakichi Hartmann

-to-

Elizabeth Blanche Walsh.

Manuscript Edition -
Limited to 160 copies
of which this is No. 116

1904, by Sadakichi Hartmann.

Instead Of A Preface.

You remember the good monk who was returning to the convent and, as he rested by the wayside beneath an oak tree, listening to the nightingale's song, fell fast asleep.

When he woke the sun was low. He stood up shivering and asked an old peasant who was passing what time it was.

"Seven o'clock," said the peasant.

"Oh, oh, then I shall not reach the monastery before nightfall."

"What monastery?" asked the surprised peasant.

"The monastery of St. Withold, two leagues from here-"

"So, ho," said the peasant, "you are one of those antiquary people, too. I thought so when I saw your odd clothes. But you are taking a useless journey - there is nothing to see, except some old stones at the gates."

"Sacked!" cried the monk, "demolished since morning -"

"Oh, long ago," said the peasant, "the father of my grandfather saw it standing - it was a hundred years ago. Since then it has been a ruin."

The good monk had slept a hundred years listening to the nightingale's song.

When I laid aside Sadakichi Hartmann's colorful pages and came down into the market place, where the books of the day are cried, I feel as composed and exceptional as the good monk of St. Withold.

And yet -

Vance Thompson.

Why I Love Thee?

      Why I love thee?
  Ask why the seawind wanders,
Why the shore is aflush with the tide,
Why the moon through heaven meanders
Like seafaring ships that ride
On a sullen, motionless deep;
    Why the seabirds are fluttering the strand
      Where the waves sing themselves to sleep
        And starshine lives in the curves of the sand!

Why I No Longer Love Thee?

     Why I no longer love thee?
   Ask why summer has fled,
Why autumn is dead with its garnet glow,
Why the sea is gray, and the sky is gray;
   Why bitter gales o'er the salt flats blow,
   Where the sea-fowl sport in ghoulish play
And the pods of the beach-pea stand withered
On the long-curved rifts of dream-torn sand;
   Why the shore is scarred by time's rough hand,
     And ships that heel on wintry seas
       Are wrecked on the ashen strand!

Nocturne.

Upon the silent sea-swept land
   The dreams of night fall soft and gray,
   The waves fade on the jeweled sand
     Like some lost hope of yesterday.

The dreams of night fall soft and gray
   Upon the summer-colored seas,
     Like some lost hope of yesterday,
     The sea-mew's song is on the breeze.

Upon the summer-colored seas
   Sails gleam and glimmer ghostly white,
     The sea-mew's song is on the breeze
   Lost in the monotone of night.

Sails gleam and glimmer ghostly white,
   They come and slowly drift away,
   Lost in the monotone of night,
     Like visions of a summer-day.

They shift and slowly drift away
　Like lovers' lays that wax and wane,
　　The visions of a summer-day
　　　Whose dreams we ne'er will dream again.

Like lovers' lays wax and wane
　The star dawn shifts from sail to sail,
　　Like dreams we ne'er will dream again;
　　　The sea-mews follow on their trail.

The star dawn shifts from sail to sail,
　As they drift to the dim unknown,
　　The sea-mews follow on their trail
　　　In quest of some dreamland zone.

In quest of some far dreamland zone,
　Of some far silent sea-swept land,
　　They are lost in the dim unknown,
　　　Where waves fade on jeweled sand
　　　　And dreams of night fall soft and gray,
　　　　　Like some lost hope of yesterday.

Drifting Flowers Of The Sea.

Across the dunes, in the waning light,
The rising moon pours her amber rays,
Through the slumbrous air of the dim, brown night
The pungent smell of the seaweed strays-
  From vast and trackless spaces
   Where wind and water meet,
    White flowers, that rise from the sleepless deep,
     Come drifting to my feet.
They flutter the shore in a drowsy tune,
  Unfurl their bloom to the lightlorn sky,
   Allow a caress to the rising moon,
    Then fall to slumber, and fade, and die.

White flowers, a-bloom on the vagrant deep,
Like dreams of love, rising out of sleep,
You are the songs, I dreamt but never sung,
Pale hopes my thoughts alone have known,
Vain words ne'er uttered, though on the tongue,
That winds to the sibilant seas have blown.
  In you, I see the everlasting drift of years
   That will endure all sorrows, smiles and tears;
    For when the bell of time will ring the doom
    To all the follies of the human race,
     You still will rise in fugitive bloom
      And garland the shores of ruined space.

Immaculate Conception.

A maiden flower stands lonesome on a vast and
 desolate plain, in trembling fear that
 her longings for life and love prove vain.

But the passing breeze takes pity, it embraces
 some flowering plant and carries its golden
 riches to the bride of the desolate land.

Windstirred she tosses her clustering hair to the
 dust of golden glow, and flower-starred with
 the waxing morn the desolate meadows grow.

A triolet.

'Tis the first day of Spring!
The catkins are a-bloom,
The bluebirds are a-wing,
'Tis the first day of Spring!
Faint scents the breezes bring;
Man's thoughts new shape assume.
'Tis the first day of Spring,
The catkins are a-bloom!

Parfum Des Fleurs.

Oh, frail and fragrant visions,
  Sweet nomads of the air,
  That rise like the mist on the meadows
  And cling to my darksome hair,

Are ye the souls of roses,
  Of memory's vagrom lays,
  Sent to caress my senses-
  Faint murmurs of bygone days?

To the "Flat Iron"

On roof and street, on park and pier,
The springtide sun shines soft and white,
Where the "Flat Iron", gaunt, austere,
Lifts its huge tiers in limpid light.

   From the city's stir and madd'ning roar
   Your monstrous shape soars in massive flight,
   And 'mid the breezes the ocean bore
   Your windows flame in the sunset light.

      Lonely and lithe, o'er the nocturnal city's
      Flickering flames, you proudly tower,
      Like some ancient, giant monolith,
      Girt with the stars and mists that lower.

All else we see fade fast and disappear,
Only your prow-like form looms gaunt, austere,
As in a sea of fog, now veiled, now clear.

   Iron structure of the time,
     Rich, in showing no pretense,
      Fair, in frugalness sublime,
   Emblem staunch of common sense,
     Well may you smile over Gotham's vast domain,
       As dawn greets your pillars with roseate flame,
         For future ages will proclaim
           Your beauty, boldly,
             Without shame.

Dawn-Flowers.
(To Maurice Maeterlinck.)

Weird phantoms rise in the dawn-wind's blow,
  In the land of shadows the dawn-flowers grow;
    The night-worn moon yields her weary glow
      To the morn-rays that over the dream-waste flow.

Oh, to know what the dawn-wind murmurs
  In chapels of pines to the ashen moons;
What the forest-well whispers to dale and dell
  With her singular, reticent runes;
To know the plaint of each falling leaf
  As it whirls across the autumnal plain;
To know the dreams of the desolate shore
  As sails, like ghosts, pass o'er the dawnlit main!
        To know, oh, to know
    Why all life's strains have the same refrain
            As of rain,
      Beating sadly against the window pane.

We do not know and we can not know,
And all that is left for us here below
(Since "songs and singers are out of date"
And the muses have met with a similar fate)
   Is to flee to the land of shadows and dreams,
      Where the dawn-flowers grow
      And the dawn-winds blow,
   As morn-rays over life's dream-waste flow
   To drown the moon in their ambient glow.

           Envoy.

Oh, gray dawn-poet of Flanders,
  Though in this life we ne'er may meet,
    I'll linger where thy dream-maids wander
      To strew these dawn-flowers at their feet.

Love By The Sea

Far away from the murmuring town,
In the region of sand and sea,
  Love has surprised us on the down-
  Love has surprised you and me-
    In this realm where sea-kissed grasses sway,
    Where winds at nightfall sadly moan,
      Where sea-gulls sing their plaintive lay.
      And waves croon in minor monotone.

No flower grows in this land of dreams,
No human habitation far or near
  Illumines the scene with a reddish gleam,
  All around is desolate and drear;
    Nothing but weeds and greyish sand-
    Yet the sea seems to say in an undertone;
      Until dawn whitens this wind-blown strand,
      The treasures of night are all thy own!

And like waves that softly shoreward creep,
Love draws us nigh as the hours pass,
  Thy fluttering hair around me sweep,
  Thy breath is like wind in the weft of the grass;
    I feel thy bosom ebb and tide -
    Its paleness resembles the moonlit sea -
      And as sea and heaven together glide
      Let thy sweetness be lost in me.

Do not be startled at the seabird's cry
Nor at the wind's relentless blast,
  Too soon the kiss on our lips will die,
  Alas, the joys of Venus never last!
    Like flowers that droop on the sunburnt sward
    Our love must needs wither and fade,
      Like blossoms that are carried seawards
      By the wind from some sleepy glade.

The joys of Venus never last,
  Love is naught but some dreamland lore,
  And as the hours are ebbing fast
   Our dream, like seaweed, will be left on the shore;
    Already the cup of the autumn moon
     Floods with her gold the distant West,
      The bitterness of life will dawn too soon,
       Forlorn lies the sea-gull's last year's nest.

             Perchance, some other autumn eve,
             May greet us on this barren wold,
             Not arm in arm, alone and fain,
             Desirous of the days of old.

Love By The Sea.

The waves have lost their silvery note,
White birds of dreams o'er the dim plain start,
Through the mist is gliding a phantom bark—
What made love open its eyes and part!

Where are the sweet names we whispered low,
Were they carried away by the breeze?
The vain words which from our lips did flow
Are they buried forever in dismal seas?
And the kisses that rained on your face
Has nothing remained of their ardent glow?
The night holds nothing but a cold embrace,
The sun of our love sank low.

Only the note of the seabird rings
  Through the dim realm of night and mist,
  Not a breath of our past love clings
  To this sea of faded amethyst.
    Even the wind pauses in space
    And refuses to caress our lips;
    Alas, our love was of fleeting pace
    Like the visions of seafaring ships.

Like the flash of a meteor's flight,-
  Know we whither its glow has flown;
  It sped across heaven with radiant light
  And vanished in worlds unknown -
    So the sweet hours have passed away
    Like flowers that on the sand-dunes grow,
    Like waves that die in a wreath of spray
    When bitter winds over the shoreland blow.

Twilight Hours

I

The colors of the rainbow are fading in the silent and distant West, and the heartache of twilight trembles within my aching breast.

For the light of my love has faded like sunbeams in the West, and the color of twilight will tremble forever in my breast.

II

I think of thy kindness often, when lonesome I feel and cold, I have not forgotten our childhood, nor your loving words of old.

And still my sweetest songs of life are floating in dreams to thee, like whisperings at eventide, across a clouded sea.

III

We two are sitting in the bark, and listen to the wavelets' play, the shore is melting in the dark, day's echoes silently decay.

Oh life, with all thy hopes so fair, wilt thou too float away, like visions rising in the air that greet the parting day!

IV

She stands amidst the roses, and tears dart from her eye that like the fragrant roses her soul must fade and die.

He stares at the twilight ocean on the shore of a foreign land, a faded rose is trembling within his soft white hand.

V

The rushes whisper softly, the sounds of silence wake,
   large flowers like sad remembrance float
   on the dark green lake.

   Were life but like the waters, so bright and calm
      and deep, and love like floating flowers
      that on the surface meet.

VI

The naked trees of autumn grope shivering through
   twilight's gloom, athwart the whispering branches
   its dying embers loom.

   I dream of life's defoliation, as I watch with
      silent dread, leaf after leaf departing, like
      hopes long withered and dead.

VII

In haunting hours of twilight dreams restless the
   turbulent sea, and heaves her white wanton
   bosom in endless mystery.

   Dream on, dream on, titanic queen, beloved sea, at
      thy wanton breast, I would find rest
      in endless mystery.

As The Lindens Shiver In Autumn Dreams.

The fields lie wrapt in autumn dreams,
  Beneath the dim, blue vault of night,
    The moon, like a bark on sluggish streams,
      Spreads soft her sail of silver light.

Beneath the blue, dim vault of night,
  With the way-worn notes of joy and care,
    Across the sea of the moon's pale light
      Dark flocks of birds flap the silent air.

With the way-worn notes of joy and care
  Fantastic shapes with wings outspread,
    Dark flocks of birds flap the silent air,
      Like a cloud of ominous dread.

Fantastic shapes with wings outspread,
  Droning some harsh and ghoulish tune,
    Like a cloud of ominous dread,
      They darken the sail of the white full moon.

They darken the sail of the soft white moon,
　　Like pageants of some Valpurgis night,
　　Droning some harsh and ghoulish tune,
　　　Their rustling wings are shimmering bright.

Their rustling wings are shimmering bright
　　As in myriad swarms they are passing by,
　　Like pageants of some Valpurgis night,
　　　Wheeling their flight to some summer sky.

Wheeling their flight whence summer has flown,
　　Like dreams and hopes now long gone by,
　　Like songs of love our youth has known,
　　　In myriad swarms they sail the sky.

· Like clouds a-sail on glassy streams -
　　Grey memories of autumn dreams;-
　　Like visions of love forever flown,
　　　You, aerial voyagers, wing your flight
　　　　To some enchanted realm our youth has known,
　　　　　Beneath the dim, blue vault of night.

Sweet Are The Dreams On The
Breeze-Blown Strand.

(Sestina Enchaînée).

When autumn cloudlets fleck the sky
  Straying southward like birds o'er the sea,
  When the flickering sunlight on the dunes
  Is pale, as seagrasses kissed by the spray,
    Seagrasses that knew the summer of yesterday-
    Sweet are the dreams on the breeze-blown strand!

Sweet are the dreams on the breeze-blown strand!
  When cloud skiffs skim athwart the sky
    And like a phantom of yesterday
    The light house shimmers out to sea
    Pale as the sand and the sea-worn spray
      And the straggling sunlight on the dunes.

Like straggling sunlight on the dunes,
  Like opal surges that wash the strand
    With briny fragrance, adoom with the spray,
    Like wander-birds that career the sky
      To flowerlit isles of some Southern sea-
      Such are the dreams of yesterday!

Alas, our dreams of yesterday,
  Frail as the fragrance of the dunes,
   Vain as dark jewels of the sea
    Cast up on some glimmering strand,
      They vanish like cloud sails on the sky,
      Pale as seagrasses frowsed by the spray.

Pale as seagrasses kissed by the spray,
　Is all this life of yesterday,
　　All our longings for clear blue skies
　　　For the low cool plash on autumn dunes,
　　All our musings on tide-left strands
　　　While birds wing southward o'er the sea.

Like birds winging southward o'er the sea
　Scattered in air-like wasteful spray,
　　Sea-fancies fading on lonesome strands
　　Weary of storm drifts of yesterday,
　　　Thus our thoughts on the sea-scooped dunes
　　　　When autumn cloudlets fleck the sky.

Oh, autumn-sea under a cloud-flecked sky
　As caressed are thy dunes with opal spray
　　So shimmer in dreams on the breeze-blown strand
　　　Sweet long-lost summers of yesterday.

Previous Works of The Author.

"Christ" - A Dramatic Poem in Three Acts.
    Author's Edition, Boston, 1893.

"Conversations with Walt Whitman"
    Author's Edition, New York, 1895.

"A Tragedy in a New York Flat" - A Dramatic Episode.
    Author's Edition, New York, 1896.

"Buddha" - A Dramatic Poem in Twelve Scenes.
    Author's Edition, New York, 1897.

"Schopenhauer in the Air"- Seven Stories.
    Author's Edition, New York, 1899.

"Shakespeare in Art" - A Compilation.
    L.C. Page & Co., Boston, 1900.

"A History of American Art" - 2 vol.
    L.C. Page & Co., Boston, 1901.
    Hutchinson & Co., London, 1903.

"Japanese Art"
    L.C. Page & Co., Boston, 1903.
    G.P. Putnam Sons, London, 1904.

Why I Publish My Own Books

Sadakichi Hartmann

I would like to say a few words of explanation in defense of the poverty-stricken make-up of my author's editions, so out of place in this modern book world of gilt edges, padding, liberal margins, and embossed covers; also of their orphan-like errantry, having no publisher's patronage to boast of, on lonesome by-paths far away from the fashionable mart.

I have published some of my books, not so much because I did not succeed in finding a publisher. I do not know whether I could (I wrote 'Christ', you know, and borrowed money rather freely without showing excessive gratitude). But aside of that, I do not particularly approve of the middleman, and I hate censorship, favoritism and intellectual boycott. I find it difficult to pirouette in the antechambers of publishing houses, and necessarily shun business transactions, lacking hustling qualities and the ability to praise up my literary ware, and furthermore, to be honest, I am conscious of an absence of tact and diplomacy in my relations with influential people: "Here are my manuscripts. You do not think favorably of them! They wouldn't please your readers. Then hand them back to me. Having waited so long, I can afford to wait a few years longer."

Not that I object to publishers, I would be only too glad to find one who would deliver me from job printers and command a larger clientele for me – but I am not inclined to go out of the way for one. If they do not realize that I would make a good business proposition, it is their shortsightedness, not mine.

Having no other aim (in my real work at least),

than to produce literature, they have no special inducements to offer. In case, one of my books should find more appreciation than I expected , and a publisher would come and say, "I would like to publish another volume of such stuff. Write it at once. I shall pay you well." I would answer, "Excuse me. I am willing to write anything you say, from an advertisement to a topical song, from an editorial to an encyclopaedia, but I can not consider this particular offer. Publish what I have on hand, I can not write anything like that on order. Besides I have planned my whole life's work and this would interfere. If you could wait five years, perhaps, I could accommodate you."

The mercenary side of literature does not interest me. I prefer to manufacture hack for any momentary material result. I do not agree with Dr. Johnson, "He is a fool who does not write for money," or with Thackeray, "We are not martyrs nor apostles, dear Barnet, but poor tradesmen working for money."

I bear no grudge against those who willingly serve as jesters for the multitude (none of us can entirely escape that fate), and get their share of kicks and coins. But I see no reason for boasting about it. Nor that I consider my writings beyond price, I am not fool enough to think that there is actually need of my writings or anybody else's. The world's literature is rich enough that it can easily dispense with the participation of most of us. I write simply because I have to, just like a tree shoots buds and bears fruit. *Ecrire ce n'est pas pour la gloire, mais pour exposer le cerveau qu'il le gene.*

The rest is futile. For my part, I wish I could afford to giveaway my books to all who care to read or own them. The mercenary spirit of our time holding the entire world spellbound taints the very best of us. Mercenary inducements invariably produce something less finished, more commonplace, and often spurious, sensational and time-pleasing, like fictile journalism and magazine literature, that are forced upon an indulgent public. The profanation of natural gifts is inexcusable , the lowest vice imaginable. Only those authors and painters who, if all opportunities of ever selling a book or picture were lost, would still continue to write and paint, are in my estimation genuine artists. In this way the amateur is frequently superior to the professional.

Literature, particularly of a quixotic, individual and experimental cast can command only a limited audience. Art patronage such as was practiced by the Medicis or by Japanese daimyos, supporting an artist for their entire life in order to let them produce one or two masterpieces, no longer exists.

Thus the author, who wants to remain true to their chosen vocation, should become their own publisher. Unless they are blessed with an income of their own... they must make the sacrifice, accept tedious office positions, toil as a hack under assumed names, maintain their independence by hook or crook, no matter how, and publish their efforts as well as they can for those few who cherish them.

The Japanese Conception of Poetry

BY SADAKICHI HARTMANN

At a time when everything in Western literature tends toward brevity of expression, it may be interesting to examine a literature which, in its poetry at least, has always adhered to the principles of concentration. Japanese poetry claims this distinction. It is absolutely confined to lyrical effusions of the utmost brevity. The Japanese poem is generally limited to 3, 4 or 5 lines, and seldom exceeds a few dozen... Japanese literature has never invaded the epic field, and knows no metrical form which even remotely resembles an ode, a ballad, or a long poetic narrative like 'The Ancient Mariner'. Also minor metrical arrangements like the rondel, triolet, villanelle, etc., are absent.

Of what, then, does Japanese poetry consist? If one discusses this... with [the] Japanese, they are sure to point to the *Man'yōshū* (*Collection of Myriad Leaves*, c. 759)... an anthology of short poems, each complete, bearing no relation to other stanzas, except in the choice of subject, extending to 122 volumes. The work [is] divided into poems of Spring, Summer, Autumn, Winter; poems of Parting, Love, Sorrow, etc. Collections of this kind, admirably printed and supplied with numerous indexes and elaborate commentaries, are published, at intervals, under the auspices of the government. They represent the classical poetry of Japan. The metrical forms most often encountered are those of the *tanka* and *haikai*.

The *tanka* is a rhythmical construction of 5 lines of 5, 7, 5, 7 and 7 syllables. To write a poem within the compass of thirty-one syllables or a dozen words... would seem to us a most difficult task. But the Japanese do not enjoy in vain the reputation of being dainty in all their æsthetic accomplishments, and the same exquisite workmanship displayed in netsuke and hammered bronzes can be found in the *tanka*. It is astonishing what a wealth of word pictures, what elegant phrasing and rhythmical shading, what subtle sentiments and almost thoughts can be compressed into these lyrical 'epigrams'. The following —a *tanka* that has won its way into the hearts of everyone —may be taken as characteristic of the vague and dreamy, and yet so suggestive style of Japanese poetry:

Moonshine! There is none:
Springtime! Where are its flowers!
Spring seems to be gone:
All life is estranged, my love
Alone has remained unchanged.

The poem explains itself. The poetess returning to the place where her lover has met her the previous spring, finds it sadly changed. As in former days the moon and the flowers greet her eyes, but in a feeling of despair she denies even their existence and plunges into melancholic musings at the sight of the familiar scenes.

The translation is as nearly as possible literal, endeavoring at the same time to imitate some rhythmical peculiarities. [For example], the original has the reiteration of 'shine' and 'time', repeats the word 'spring' in the third line, and has the same ending for the second and third line. Any attempt, however, to convey the euphony and the rhythmic beauty of a Japanese poem into a foreign tongue, is futile... Measure [and] rhyming in our Western sense is unknown...

The only ambition of the *tanka* writer is to make every poem a rhythmic whole, an expression of fresh and unconscious modulation. The subject itself—be it a wall of rippling wistaria or the undulations of a tree trunk—has to suggest the rhythm most suitable for the interpretation. And as the open vowel sounds permit an endless variety of modulation, and as there are no metrical rules, it is really nothing but a 'primitive' application of *vers libre*...

And yet in a way nothing more perfect and complete than these little poems can be imagined. The alternation of lines of 5 and 7 syllables, the improvisation of a rhythm, and the exclusive application of the so-called 'classic' style, which prohibits words of Chinese derivation and all colloquial expressions, are obeyed scrupulously. There has never existed a word-arrangement which, despite its apparent looseness, has remained so firm in construction and so decided in purpose through centuries of use.

The leading characteristic of the Japanese poet seems to be their fertile fancy for pictorial minuteness. Nature is always the leading motif. All metaphors are drawn from the external beauties of nature. The moon is a bark oaring its way to the grove of the stars; sporting butterflies resemble fallen flowers that return to their branches; the poet wishes that the white breakers far out on the sea were flowers that would drift to their love; and asks the fir-clad cliffs at the seashore how many wet wave-garments they have worn. The sight of two old fir-trees suggests to them a married couple growing old together. They never tire of depicting the four seasons in all their aspects... Nearly everything in nature interests them. The hazes and 'ice thaws' which usher in the spring, the sound of falling leaves on an autumn evening, the sough of wind in the reeds at the edge of the marshes, the vision of the snow-covered summits of Fuji, or of fir-clad cliffs glimmering out to sea, are some of the subjects the Japanese poet likes to dwell upon.

There is no flower blooming in Japan which has not received adequate poetic treatment, and one might assert that at least 1/4 of all poems mention either the cherry-flowers, the wisteria, the peony, the convolvulus, or the vari-colored blossoms of the plum-tree which exhale their perfume in the snow and frost and "make us think longingly of the past." Like the Japanese painter, who excels in expressing the attitudes and motion of fish and fowl, and, above all, the sportive grace of little forest creatures, like the squirrel, the poet also finds inspiration in the leaping of a trout in a mountain stream, the lines of wild geese making a dark streak across the sky, even in the croaking of a frog among lotus leaves, or the chirruping of insects in the undergrowth.

For centuries the *tanka* which, according to Japanese belief was already in use in prehistoric times, reigned supreme. It had caught the ear of the public, and apparently satisfied all lyrical aspirations. No innovation was attempted. At last in the 16th century a serious rival, in the shape of a still shorter poem, the *haikai*, made its appearance. If the term lyrical 'epigram' is appropriate for the brevity and metrical limitations of the *tanka*, the *haikai* should be called a 'lyrical aphorism'...

17 syllables—3 lines of 5, 7, 5 syllables—are all the resources a writer has to produce a word-picture... and there are actually poems of this kind which consist merely of 4 or 5 words. Moreover, a certain compound adjective, the 'pillow word', is used, a survival from the archaic stages of the language. The mountains are 'mist-enshrouded', or 'dotted-with-monasteries', the fall moon [is] 'soul-contenting', the cherry blossoms 'drenched-with-spring-rain', etc. And as these epithets convey to the native reader a deeper meaning than meets our ear, and as these words are invariably 5 words long, they form a most valuable vehicle for concise expression.

The *haikai*, however, differs from the tanka in more than the number of lines. It is less [refined] in diction, and deals at times with humorous and frivolous subjects, which the older poetry refuses to meddle with. But it enriched the [poetic] vocabulary by the adoption of large numbers of Chinese words, and acquired a clearness and directness unattainable with the more cumbersome expressions of the classical style. A typical *haikai* is the following one:

> A cloud of flowers!
> Is it Ueno's bell
> Or Asakusa's?

To the Japanese student these lines convey a perfect picture. The famous temples of Ueno and Asakusa in the vicinity of Edo are surrounded by a belt of cherry-trees, whose blossoms form a perfect wall in spring, shutting them entirely out of view. And the passer-by does not know whether the bell of Ueno or Asakusa is ringing. Suggestiveness like this can hardly be excelled. Nothing but the most essential is expressed. It is very much like the Japanese [painter], who expresses by one dash of their brush a swallow in full flight, or suggests, by an angle of lines with a half-circle behind, the autumn moon rising among the hills. To our Western mind this impressionism which seems more remarkable for what it does not represent than what it does, is often obscurely allusive. It transcends our comprehension. We want passages of pathos that draw tears, sublime utterances that overawe our soul... We want a finished picture—not a vision without shadows and perspective—a 'true' poetic expression, quite independent of the verbal melody, perfectly expressed in regard to style and form.

The Japanese reader agrees with us that emotion is the true basis of all poetic expression, but they want merely a suggestion to convey to the sketchy outlines of the poet's conception their own poetic imagination, and the emotions that are stirred within their own breast. How much confidence the Japanese poet has in their readers is astonishing. Frequently they do not even find it necessary to attach a sentiment to their word-pictures. They simply depict a crow sitting on a withered branch, and leave it to the reader to add the poetic thought. If they want to dwell upon the fugitiveness of all earthly things they simply say, 'A joint of bamboo is floating down the river'; if they want to compare the sorrows of people with fading autumn leaves that cover the ground, they exclaim, 'There are far more of you that I ever saw growing on the trees!' And the melancholic despair of two lovers, whose passion has subsided, they express by a single image. When the lovers' passion was at its height, they swore they would love each other as long as the smoke should rise from Mt. Fuji. The poet, however, deems it unnecessary to make this explanation, find[ing] it amply sufficient to express this complex emotion, to which Swinburne has devoted hundreds of lines... by one short, sharply-defined sentence, 'The smoke no longer rises from Mt. Fuji'.

The symbolism of Japanese poetry is unique. It has nothing in common with our Western emblematic signs and forms. It is rather a spiritual idea, a subtle speculation, a unison of the external beauties of nature and the subtleties of the human soul, which has its origin in tradition and a continual association with flowers, with animals, trees, and mountains, and the ever changing elements. Every glimpse of nature is endowed with symbol, a hidden meaning to all who know the magic pass-word. In this graphic symbolism exists for the initiated the greatest charm of Japanese poetry. It may be interesting to investigate how this singular terseness, this love for reduction, condensation and fragmentary beauty, came into Japanese literature.

The writing of [*tanka* was] no profession in Japan. The poets were mostly courtiers or ladies of the leisure class, who took up verse-making as a pastime. Nearly every 'well bred' person can improvise a *tanka*...

Much of the poetry was the outcome of poetic tournaments, at which themes were proposed by judges; and each phrase and word was examined with the minutest care before the verdict was pronounced. And as hundreds of poets and poetesses took part in these competitions, of which two were held annually at the imperial court, it can be imagined that short poems were in favor... To them [poetry] was... a substitute for a cup of thick sake, or for the few whiffs of which Japanese smoke consists. They looked at literature as a sport... a game like any other... They merely wished to lend expression to a passing fancy, and they found the *tanka* a most suitable form. The subtlety of sentiment is largely due to feminine participation [and] a large part of Japanese poetry was written by women.

Writing for leisure and guided by an exquisite taste, they never published their effusions—volumes of poetry by an individual writer are almost unknown—leaving the responsibility of selection to the government, which took pride in issuing anthologies. The poet was apparently of the opinion that the 'less literary baggage they took with them the more certain they were of traveling safely down the roads of fame'.

[Finally], three other metrical forms still have to be investigated. They are the *nagauta* (the 'long poem'), the *hanka* (a sort of envoi attached to other poems), and the *kyōka* (the comic verse). The *nagauta* are very scarce. The *Kokinshū* (c. 914), an anthology of over 1100 ancient and modern poems, contains only 5 specimens... The *hanka* is a short poem of 31 syllables in 5 lines [ed.]. It is never used as an independent poem, but invariably as a feature of the long poem. Unlike the envoi, it is not addressed to any art patron, high dignitary or symbolic personage, but is in most cases simply an echo of the principle idea of the poem, or a commentary on the leading event or character. The *kyōka* is a variety of the *tanka*. Its principle object is to make people laugh, and absolute liberties in regard to language and choice of subjects are taken. The language, although irresistibly funny... is often extremely improper. Ordinary poems and acrostics, pillow-words and pivot-words [i.e. a word which has 2 meanings, and is used in a way that makes sense with the preceding sentence, as well as the following], and other contortions of speech are used with an exasperating lavishness.

The introduction of Western ideas has also changed Japanese poetry to some extent. The study of Western literature was introduced, and Shakespeare, Gray, Campbell, Longfellow, and other poets have been translated in parts... A 'new school' of poetry, which took up European and American writers as models sprang up in the 1880s. They [returned to] *nagauta*, but divide them like our ballads into stanzas of equal length... Finding the classical language [of poetry] unequal to the expression of new ideas, they make free use of the colloquial, which hitherto had only been used in the *kyōka* [and *haikai*]... Although the *tanka* and *haikai* are still the most favored and characteristic forms, it cannot be denied that the [recent] movements have endowed Japanese poetry with new and rich resources. If, without abandoning the modern standpoint it will still be able to adhere to its classic principles, to the truthfulness of its similes and metaphors, to its love of nature and free and spontaneous expression of emotion, the all-pervading suggestiveness of Japanese art will speak to us with renewed vigor and with more eloquence than it hitherto has spoken.

> *This Space for Your Thoughts*

PUBLICDOMAINPOETS.COM

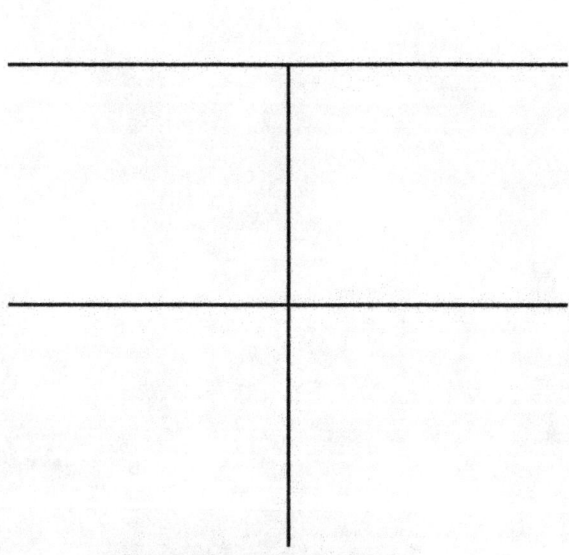

Please handle with care.

www.ingramcontent.com/pod-product-compliance
Lightning Source LLC
Chambersburg PA
CBHW022123040426
42450CB00006B/824